EARTHS EPIC START

COSTI & CHRISTYNE HINN

HARVEST
Kids

HARVEST HOUSE PUBLISHERS
EUGENE, OREGON

To our precious children,
May your desire to study God's Word
increase with each day.

We love you,
Dad and Mom

Published in association with the literary agency of Wolgemuth & Wilson.

Cover, interior design, and illustrations by Juicebox Designs.
Author photo by Titus Hinn.

For bulk, special sales, or ministry purchases, please call 1-800-547-8979. Email: CustomerService@hhpbooks.com

 This logo is a federally registered trademark of the Hawkins Children's LLC. Harvest House Publishers, Inc., is the exclusive licensee of this trademark.

Earth's Epic Start
Copyright © 2025 by Costi Hinn and Christyne Hinn
Published by Harvest House Publishers
Eugene, Oregon 97408
www.harvesthousepublishers.com

ISBN 978-0-7369-8980-0 (pbk.)

Printed in China

25 26 27 28 29 30 31 32 33 / DC / 10 9 8 7 6 5 4 3 2 1

CONTENTS

EPIC FROM THE START

Your view of creation will be one of the most important aspects of a *Christian worldview* that you will develop in these early years of your life. For those of you asking, "What is a Christian worldview?"—we are so glad you asked! A Christian worldview is a view of the world that matches the way God and the Bible view the world. We find all our answers to life's biggest questions and direction from God's Word.

The facts we're going to discover about creation will give you confidence that the God you believe in and the Bible you read are real and true! Most importantly, you're going to be taking big-time steps toward knowing how to study the Bible all by yourself.

Just like building a house requires tools and knowledge of how to use those tools, building a strong foundation for understanding creation starts with several key tools.

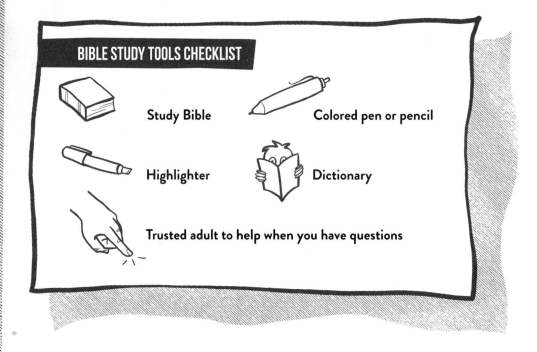

BIBLE STUDY TOOLS CHECKLIST

Study Bible

Colored pen or pencil

Highlighter

Dictionary

Trusted adult to help when you have questions

HOW TO USE THE STUDY

Have fun doing this Bible study for six days, and rest on the seventh day just like God did when He created the world.

 Start each day with prayer.

 Read the verses for each day's study. As you read, mark up the Scripture using the directions in the list below called "Suggestions for using your tools."

 Complete the questions for each day.

 Practice your memory verse and ask someone to test you. There are memory verse cards in the back of the study for you to cut out and practice.

SUGGESTIONS FOR USING YOUR TOOLS:

HIGHLIGHT who, what, where, and events.

CIRCLE any words you do not know so you can look them up.

UNDERLINE important phrases and repetitive words.

QUESTION MARKS should be put next to anything confusing or to note questions you may have.

Then write down specific questions in the provided note-taking space on day 4 of each week's study.

HERE IS AN EXAMPLE OF HOW YOUR STUDY NOTES MIGHT LOOK FOR ONE SECTION OF BIBLE VERSES:

Genesis 1: 1-2

before anything
time begins
made from nothing

In the beginning, God created the heavens and the earth. ² The earth was without form and void, and

Holy Spirit

darkness was over the face of the deep. And the Spirit of God was hovering over the face of the waters.

Does this mean ocean?

Note to parents: If your child is still too young to read everything in this study, then we suggest you complete the study together. Make it interesting! One of my daughters and I often have a simple tea party while we study the Bible together. Another thing, be available! With six children, we definitely know it can be difficult at times, but imparting biblical truth to our children should be our main goal. (See Deuteronomy 6:7...we're reminding ourselves of this too!)

GOAL OF THIS STUDY

Goals give us something to aim for so we can get the most out of studying God's word. Let's set some goals for this study of Genesis!

- To know God in a deeper way by understanding that He is the One behind EVERYTHING.

- To grow your knowledge of how He created everything. This will create a sense of awe and glory directed to the Lord. It will also allow you to share with others how amazing God is.

- Most importantly, have fun! Learning about creation, the Fall, and our future to come can change your life forever!

So what are we waiting for? Let's get started!

AUTHOR OF GENESIS: MOSES

★ Genesis is called the book of Moses (Joshua 8:31, Joshua 23:6, 2 Kings 14:6, Ezra 6:18, Nehemiah 13:1, Daniel 9:11, Mark 12:26).

★ God commanded Moses to write a testimony in a book (Exodus 17:14, Numbers 33:2, 1 Chronicles 22:13, Malachi 4:4, Luke 24:44).

★ Moses was trained to write. He received an excellent education as he was raised in the royal palace in Egypt (Acts 7:22).

★ Moses was a prophet who wrote the Pentateuch (the first five books of the Bible: Genesis, Exodus, Leviticus, Numbers, Deuteronomy) through divine inspiration (2 Timothy 3:16).

WHEN IT WAS WRITTEN

Here is a fun timeline of when key events in the Bible took place:

☾ **Creation:** 4000 BC

☾ **First sin:** soon after creation was complete, 4000 BC

☾ **Exiled from garden:** soon after Adam and Eve sinned, 4000 BC

☾ **Book of Genesis:** written between 1445–1405 BC

☾ **Jesus's birth:** 4–6 BC

☾ **Jesus's death:** 30–33 AD

☾ **Jesus's resurrection:** 30–33 AD, three days after His death

☾ **Jesus's return:** "I (Jesus) am coming soon" (Revelation 22:12)

WEEK 1

GENESIS 1:1-5

Have you ever made something from scratch? Maybe you've baked a cake or built a fort using certain ingredients or materials to make your masterpiece! Well, when God created the universe, He made it out of absolutely nothing! That's right, with no ingredients or building materials to start with, He supernaturally made everything by His own power. Unlike humans, God is divine and capable of creating every atom, molecule, cell, and organism without any help. He didn't make trees from wood, He made the trees from nothing, and that's how we have wood! He never had to go to the store or ask the angels to bring Him supplies. He simply spoke creation into existence by the power of His word. Psalm 33:6 tells us, "By the word of the LORD the heavens were made, and by the breath of his mouth all their host."

In our study this week, we're going to memorize verses that will help us remember how powerful God is and how He started the universe. We'll get a front row seat to the first day ever made. We'll learn how God created light and got our universe off and running with an epic start!

| PRAY. | READ to understand, rather than race to the finish. | HIGHLIGHT who, what, and where. | CIRCLE key words and phrases you do not understand. | Add QUESTION MARKS next to anything confusing. | UNDERLINE important phrases and repetitive words. |

What is a KEY WORD?

A key word is an **important** word. When we see key words, we want to stop and make sure we know what they mean, because they often help you better understand the section you're reading. Key words will be bold and underlined throughout the study. The key words are listed on pages 92-93, and you will find them marked in the book with this symbol.

GENESIS 1:1-5

¹ In the beginning, God created the heavens and the earth. ² The earth was without form and void, and darkness was over the face of the deep. And the Spirit of God was hovering over the face of the waters. ³ And God said, "Let there be light," and there was light. ⁴ And God saw that the light was good. And God separated the light from the darkness. ⁵ God called the light Day, and the darkness he called Night. And there was evening and there was morning, the first day.

NOTES

DAY 2

Choose at least one verse to memorize this week.

For a cutout card of each memory verse, see pages 95-96 at the back of this study.

MEMORY VERSE

☐ In the beginning, God created the heavens and the earth (Genesis 1:1).

☐ And God saw everything that he had made, and behold, it was very good (Genesis 1:31).

Read Genesis 1:1-5 again and fill in the following sections.

WORDS TO /lŏŏk·úp/

_____ : _____

_____ : _____

_____ : _____

¿?
WHAT HAPPENED?

_____

_____

_____

HOW DID IT HAPPEN?

_____

_____

Did you know? God created everything out of nothing!

Yes, that's right. The word 🔑 **created** means to "make something new" and God made a brand-new creation. The Hebrew word for God is 🔑 **Elohim**. The name Elohim is found 32 times in chapter 1. Elohim means "mighty and powerful one." Only a mighty God could create a whole universe out of nothing!

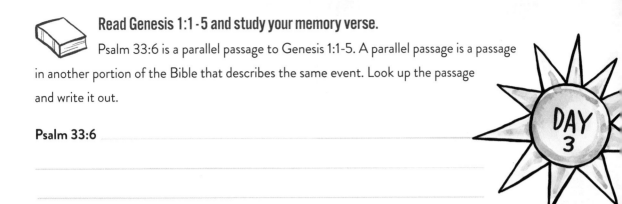

Read Genesis 1:1-5 and study your memory verse.

Psalm 33:6 is a parallel passage to Genesis 1:1-5. A parallel passage is a passage in another portion of the Bible that describes the same event. Look up the passage and write it out.

Psalm 33:6 _____

_____

_____

God truly is amazing, having created everything with a perfect design.
Here are just five of God's attributes we can see in creation.

- **ETERNAL: God has no beginning or end** (Psalm 90:2).

- **GOOD: God is the standard for good and everything He does is good** (Luke 18:19).

- **LOVING: God is love. His love is unchanging and eternal** (1 John 4:8).

- **OMNIPOTENT: God is all-powerful. He can do anything He wills** (Jeremiah 32:27).

- **OMNISCIENT: God is all-knowing. He knows everything** (Psalm 139:1-2).

Read Genesis 1:2 again.

 Hovered is a Hebrew word that means "a gentle flutter."

Who was "hovering over the face of the waters"? _____

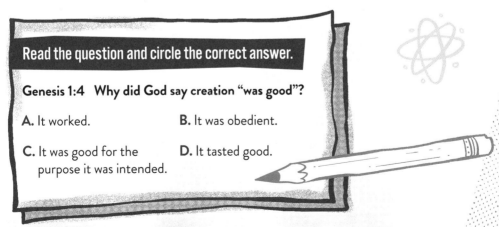

Read the question and circle the correct answer.

Genesis 1:4   Why did God say creation "was good"?

A. It worked.

B. It was obedient.

C. It was good for the purpose it was intended.

D. It tasted good.

 Read Genesis 1:1-5 and study your memory verse.

Use this section to write down questions you may have from this week's passage:

 Use this section to write down answers to your questions. Ask for help if needed.

Draw a line to connect the items on the left with the matching words on the right. See this week's passage for help.

light   hovered over the waters

Spirit of God   day

darkness   formless and void

earth   night

Read Genesis 1:1-5 and study your memory verse.

Look at the word *beginning* and the description of the earth in verses 1:1-2 and notice how God brought the universe to life out of nothing! For example, He made everything big and small, from the largest planet to the tiniest atom. To describe this, we use the Latin phrase ***ex nihilo***, meaning "out of nothing."

DAY 5

Genesis 1:4 What did God see that the light was? _____

Genesis 1:5 When did time begin? _____

Read the question and circle the correct answer.

Genesis 1:5 What length of time is described by "there was evening and there was morning"?

A. 12 hours   **B.** 3 days

C. 1 million years   **D.** 24 hours

"I am the Alpha and the Omega," says the Lord God, "who is and who was and who is to come" (Revelation 1:8). ***Alpha*** and ***Omega*** mean beginning and end. God is what we call eternal.

Eternal means He has no beginning and no end. Why do you think this is important for us to know?

ALPHA & OMEGA

_____
_____
_____
_____

Read Genesis 1:1-5 and study your memory verse.
Without looking, write down your memory verse.

_____

_____

_____

Did you know God the Father, God the Son, and God the Holy Spirit were all part of creation? Who is the Spirit of God in verse 2? _____

Find and circle these words in the word search below:

beginning	formed	holy	night
creator	God	hovering	power
day	good	light	Spirit
earth	heavens	Jesus	righteous

```
S  U  H  J  I  Z  J  C  J  M  E  D  Z  Q  B  W  H  N
R  W  B  S  P  N  N  S  A  U  Z  H  R  Y  L  O  H  V
E  Y  Z  U  A  Z  F  Q  W  E  R  T  Y  U  V  C  S  Y
W  I  A  O  P  G  K  L  T  R  O  T  A  E  R  C  U  M
O  A  S  E  D  F  J  H  K  L  M  N  R  B  C  X  S  N
P  T  U  T  P  L  G  O  O  D  W  I  R  T  Y  R  E  B
S  D  H  H  F  I  H  J  L  C  N  S  B  N  M  E  J  V
A  S  D  G  N  I  N  N  I  G  E  B  N  R  E  T  Z  C
D  F  G  I  I  C  J  R  S  W  E  O  P  E  I  L  C  O
A  W  A  R  K  L  E  M  S  P  O  L  U  A  V  N  B  S
Y  A  D  D  S  P  R  I  Y  A  I  N  I  S  G  A  L  E
E  R  O  B  N  M  C  K  L  F  O  R  M  E  D  W  E  X
T  R  G  H  T  R  A  E  Y  Z  P  O  I  B  L  J  K  H
C  L  Q  U  I  F  L  P  B  N  M  B  X  T  Y  H  G  F
```

Read the question and circle the correct answer.

Psalm 148:5   Why is it important that God spoke creation into being?

A. God was the first example of speaking.

B. It shows His power and authority. No one can speak anything into existence except God.

C. Words are important.

D. It just is.

EX NIHILO

"OUT OF NOTHING"

On the seventh day, "God rested from all his work" (Genesis 2:3). You've worked so hard this week—go and do the same!

DAY 7

ANSWER KEY

Here are some important answers to questions in the book. If an answer is not listed here, use your Bible to find the answer, or answer the question in your own words.

DAY 6: *The Spirit of God is:* the Holy Spirit   *Multiple Choice:*   B

DAY 5: *Light was:* Good   *Time began:* on the first day   *Multiple Choice:* D   ◊

DAY 4: *Draw a line:* light » day; Spirit of God » hovered; darkness » night; earth » formless   ◊

WEEK 1   DAY 3: *Who was hovering?* The Spirit of God (or the Holy Spirit)   *Multiple Choice:* C   ◊

WEEK 2

GENESIS 1:6-8

DAY 1

Have you ever heard of the famous painting called the *Mona Lisa*? It was painted by Leonardo Da Vinci sometime between 1503 and 1519—no one knows for sure! But what we do know is that it's considered the most expensive painting in the world because of its beauty and rareness. It's worth a whopping 860 million dollars! Another painting among the most expensive and beautiful in the world is in the Vatican. It's on the ceiling of the Sistine Chapel and is priceless because it can never be sold! Michelangelo was the famous artist who painted the Sistine Chapel and today, millions of people go see it every single year. Guess how long it took him to paint it? Four years! That's right, he labored from 1508 to 1512 to make his masterpiece and it still wows people over 500 years later. Think about how awesome and valuable paintings are from history, and still, God's masterpiece in the sky makes them all look like preschool finger-painting projects.

Have you ever looked up at puffy clouds and bright blue sky and wondered, *How in the world did that masterpiece get there?* Well, the Bible teaches that it all began with day 2 of creation when God separated the waters to create the sky, leaving water below that would eventually become the sea (on day 3). Considering how massive the sky is, it's incredible to think that God is bigger than all of it. Psalm 95:3-7 reminds us, "The LORD is a great God, and a great King above all gods. In his hand are the depths of the earth." He formed everything perfectly, a masterpiece that is better than any expensive painting.

| PRAY. | READ to understand, rather than race to the finish. | HIGHLIGHT who, what, and where. | CIRCLE key words and phrases you do not understand. | Add QUESTION MARKS next to anything confusing. | UNDERLINE important phrases and repetitive words. |

GENESIS 1:6-8

[6] And God said, "Let there be an expanse in the midst of the waters, and let it separate the waters from the waters." [7] And God made the expanse and separated the waters that were under the expanse from the waters that were above the expanse. And it was so. [8] And God called the expanse Heaven. And there was evening and there was morning, the second day.

NOTES

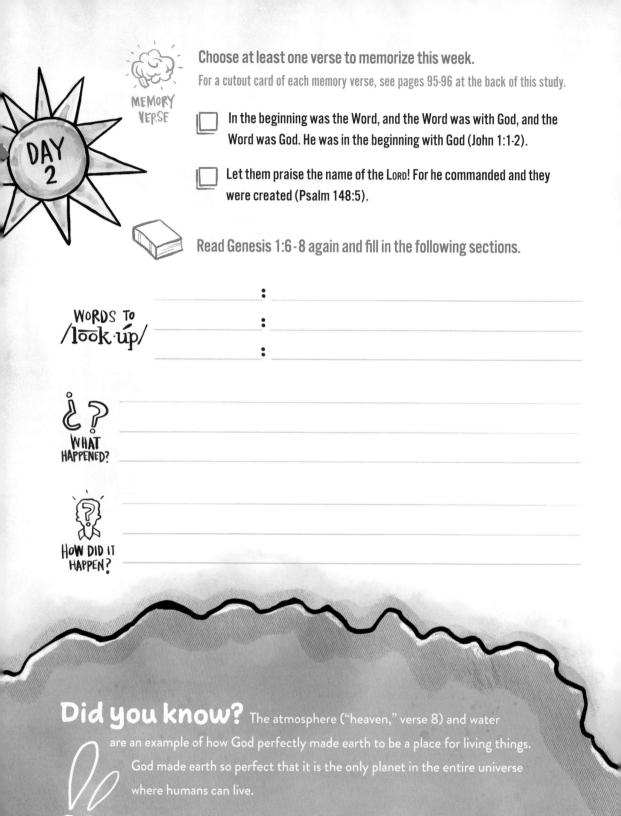

DAY 2

MEMORY VERSE

Choose at least one verse to memorize this week.

For a cutout card of each memory verse, see pages 95-96 at the back of this study.

☐ In the beginning was the Word, and the Word was with God, and the Word was God. He was in the beginning with God (John 1:1-2).

☐ Let them praise the name of the Lord! For he commanded and they were created (Psalm 148:5).

Read Genesis 1:6-8 again and fill in the following sections.

WORDS TO /lŏŏk·úp/

:

:

:

¿? WHAT HAPPENED?

HOW DID IT HAPPEN?

Did you know? The atmosphere ("heaven," verse 8) and water are an example of how God perfectly made earth to be a place for living things. God made earth so perfect that it is the only planet in the entire universe where humans can live.

Read Genesis 1: 6-8 and study your memory verse.

Psalm 33:8-9 and Jeremiah 10:12 are parallel passages to Genesis 1:6-8.

Look up each passage and write it out.

Psalm 33:8-9 _____

_____

_____

Jeremiah 10:12 _____

_____

_____

Jeremiah 10:12 **God created using these three things:**

1. _____

2. _____

3. _____

Think of a time when you were in awe of God's creation.
Use the space below to recreate what you saw.

Read Genesis 1:6-8 and study your memory verse.

Use this section to write down questions you may have from this week's passage:

_____

_____

_____

_____

_____

Use this section to write down answers to your questions. Ask for help if needed.

_____

_____

_____

_____

_____

_____

Read Job 38:8-11 and fill in the blanks.

Or who _____ in the sea with doors when it burst out from the _____ , when I made

_____ its garment and thick darkness its _____ band, and _____

limits for it and set _____ and doors, and said, "Thus far shall you come, and no

_____ , and here shall your _____ waves be stayed"?

Read Genesis 1:6-8 and study your memory verse.
Use your dictionary to define the word *expanse*.

_____

_____

_____

What was created on the second day of creation?

_____

_____

_____

We are to take the whole Bible literally and read it
as if God is directly saying each word to us.

Read 2 Timothy 3:16 and fill in the blanks.

All Scripture is _____ _____ by God.

Genesis 1:14   **Explain: How do you know each day is a literal 24 hours?**

_____

_____

_____

**Read Genesis 1:6-8 and study your memory verse.
Without looking, write down your memory verse.**

DAY
6

_____

_____

_____

_____

Psalm 33:9   Why is it significant that God spoke creation into being?

_____

_____

_____

_____

Romans 1:20   What invisible attributes can be seen in creation?

_____

_____

_____

_____

Psalm 19:1   How does the sky remind you of God's character?

_____

_____

_____

_____

On the seventh day, "God rested from all his work" (Genesis 2:3). You've worked so hard this week—go and do the same!

ANSWER KEY

Here are some important answers to questions in the book. If an answer is not listed here, use your Bible to find the answer, or answer the question in your own words.

WEEK 2 **DAY 5: Expanse:** a wide or great area of something spread out. *Genesis 1:14* tells us, "There was evening and there was morning, the first day." This means that we are to take literally to mean each day is 24 hours and consists of one evening and morning. ◇ **DAY 6:** *Psalm 33:9* It shows His power and authority over all things. *Romans 1:20* His eternal power and divine nature.

WEEK 3

DAY 1

What do front yard trees, baseball fields, garden vegetables, surfing, and beach volleyball all have in common? They are all made possible because of God's power, which we will study in this week's passage! "It is he who made the earth by his power, who established the world by his wisdom, and by his understanding stretched out the heavens" (Jeremiah 10:12). Genesis 1:9-13 showcases God's creativity and power as He established the oceans, dry land, plants, trees, fruits, and vegetables. Next time you plant a flower, enjoy the beach, or eat fresh fruit, you can thank God for His amazing creation!

PRAY.

READ to understand, rather than race to the finish.

HIGHLIGHT who, what, and where.

CIRCLE key words and phrases you do not understand.

Add QUESTION MARKS next to anything confusing.

UNDERLINE important phrases and repetitive words.

[9] And God said, "Let the waters under the heavens be gathered together into one place, and let the dry land appear." And it was so. [10] God called the dry land Earth, and the waters that were gathered together he called Seas. And God saw that it was good. [11] And God said, "Let the earth sprout vegetation, plants yielding seed, and fruit trees bearing fruit in which is their seed, each according to its kind, on the earth." And it was so. [12] The earth brought forth vegetation, plants yielding seed according to their own kinds, and trees bearing fruit in which is their seed, each according to its kind. And God saw that it was good. [13] And there was evening and there was morning, the third day.

NOTES

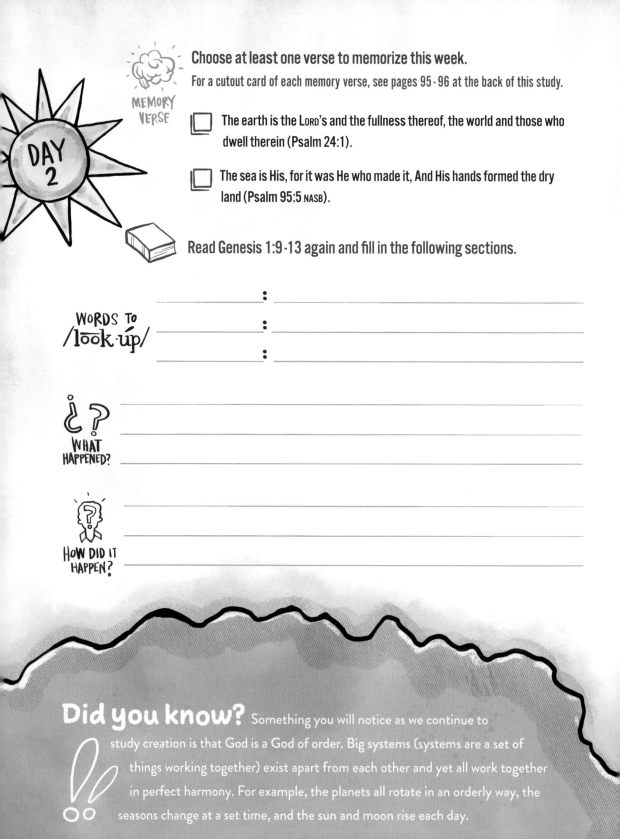

DAY 2

MEMORY VERSE

Choose at least one verse to memorize this week.

For a cutout card of each memory verse, see pages 95-96 at the back of this study.

☐ The earth is the Lord's and the fullness thereof, the world and those who dwell therein (Psalm 24:1).

☐ The sea is His, for it was He who made it, And His hands formed the dry land (Psalm 95:5 NASB).

Read Genesis 1:9-13 again and fill in the following sections.

WORDS TO /look·úp/

_____ : _____

_____ : _____

_____ : _____

¿?
WHAT HAPPENED?

?
HOW DID IT HAPPEN?

Did you know? Something you will notice as we continue to study creation is that God is a God of order. Big systems (systems are a set of things working together) exist apart from each other and yet all work together in perfect harmony. For example, the planets all rotate in an orderly way, the seasons change at a set time, and the sun and moon rise each day.

Read Genesis 1:9-13 and study your memory verse.

Psalm 95:5 and 2 Peter 3:5 are parallel passages to Genesis 1:9-13.
Look up each passage and write it out.

Psalm 95:5 _____

_____

_____

_____

DAY
3

2 Peter 3:5 _____

_____

_____

_____

Read Psalm 104:24-25 and fill in the blanks.

O Lord, how _____ are your works! In _____ have you

made them all; the earth is full of your _____. Here is the sea, great

and wide, which teems with creatures _____ , living things both

_____ and great.

Psalm 19:1-3   How are we to respond to God's creation?

_____

_____

_____

_____

_____

Read Genesis 1:9-13 and study your memory verse.

Use this section to write down questions you may have from this week's passage:

_____

_____

_____

_____

Use this section to write down answers to your questions. Ask for help if needed.

_____

_____

_____

Genesis 1:12   What do you think "brought forth vegetation, plants yielding seed according to their own kinds, and trees bearing fruit in which is their seed, each according to its kind" means?

_____

_____

_____

What is something you find fascinating about creation?

_____

_____

_____

Read Genesis 1:9-13 and study your memory verse.

Psalm 104:9 Explain: What did God do with the waters on day 3 of creation?

_____

_____

_____

DAY 5

Unscramble the words below in Isaiah 45:12 and use them to fill in the blanks.

rahet   nam   ehtrestcd   aevsneh   medmocand

I made the _____ and created _____ on it; it was my hands

that _____ out the _____ , and I

_____ all their host. Isaiah 45:12

Draw some images of God's creation on day 3:

Read Genesis 1:9-13 and study your memory verse. Without looking, write down your memory verse.

DAY 6

_____

_____

_____

_____

Genesis 1:10   God called the dry land _____ , and the waters that were gathered together He called _____ .

Why do you think God made the plants before animals?

_____

_____

_____

_____

_____

_____

Genesis 1:2   What did God use to create everything?

_____

_____

_____

_____

_____

On the seventh day, "God rested from all his work" (Genesis 2:3).
You've worked so hard this week—go and do the same!

ANSWER KEY

Here are some important answers to questions in the book. If an answer is not listed here, use your Bible to find the answer, or answer the question in your own words.

WEEK 3   DAY 4: *Genesis 1:12* It means they were able to reproduce more of their own kind of fruit. A daisy could not reproduce an apple tree.   ◇ **DAY 5:** *Psalm 104:9* He created boundaries (land). *Unscramble:* earth; man; stretched; heavens; commanded   ◇ **DAY 6:** *Genesis 1:2* Nothing. He spoke everything into creation.

WEEK 4

DAY 1

One of the wildest facts about creation is how massive the universe is. We don't often think about this because all we see are the neighborhoods we live in, the sky above our heads, or the mountains in the distance. But the universe that God created reflects His glory, majesty, and power. It is so vast, human beings have not explored even a fraction of it! Take for example, the stars. Did you know that the closest star to earth is Proxima Centauri, and it is 4.24 light-years away? A *light-year* is how long it takes for something to travel at the speed of light. One light-year is 9.44 trillion kilometers (5.88 trillion miles). Even though it's the nearest star, Proxima Centauri is so far away that walking to it would take 950 million years!

When we think about just one star that God made, and then consider that we have discovered over 80 million stars in the universe, it blows our minds to think of how huge the universe is. Now imagine this: No matter how big the universe is, God is even bigger! Let's always remember how much bigger and greater God is than us! Isaiah 55:8-9 is a great reminder, "For my thoughts are not your thoughts, neither are your ways my ways, declares the LORD. For as the heavens are higher than the earth, so are my ways higher than your ways and my thoughts than your thoughts."

In this week's study, we're learning about the day that God created the sun, moon, and stars. With what He created, the sky lights up with beauty both day and night.

| PRAY. | READ to understand, rather than race to the finish. | HIGHLIGHT who, what, and where. | CIRCLE key words and phrases you do not understand. | Add QUESTION MARKS next to anything confusing. | UNDERLINE important phrases and repetitive words. |

GENESIS 1:14-19

[14] And God said, "Let there be lights in the expanse of the heavens to separate the day from the night. And let them be for signs and for seasons, and for days and years, [15] and let them be lights in the expanse of the heavens to give light upon the earth." And it was so. [16] And God made the two great lights—the greater light to rule the day and the lesser light to rule the night—and the stars. [17] And God set them in the expanse of the heavens to give light on the earth, [18] to rule over the day and over the night, and to separate the light from the darkness. And God saw that it was good. [19] And there was evening and there was morning, the fourth day.

NOTES

_____

_____

_____

_____

_____

DAY 2

For a cutout card of each memory verse, see pages 95-96 at the back of this study.

MEMORY VERSE

Choose at least one verse to memorize this week.

☐ Let there be lights in the expanse of the heavens to separate the day from the night. And let them be for signs and for seasons, and for days and years (Genesis 1:14).

☐ To him who made the great lights, for his steadfast love endures forever (Psalm 136:7).

Read Genesis 1:14-19 again and fill in the following sections.

WORDS TO /lŏŏk·úp/

_____ : _____
_____ : _____
_____ : _____

WHAT HAPPENED?

_____
_____
_____

HOW DID IT HAPPEN?

_____
_____
_____

Did you know? Historically, people had to look up to the heavens to determine the time and date. Seasons were a part of God's original creation. For extra fun, go outside and look at the placement of the sun. Try to test yourself to see if you can tell what time it is. *Do not look directly at the sun. It will damage your eyes.* The sun is usually in the highest position when it is noon. Did you know that the stars also rise from the east and set in the west?

Read Genesis 1:14-19 and study your memory verse.

Jeremiah 31:35 and Psalm 136:7-9 are parallel passages to Genesis 1:14-19.

Look up each passage and write it out.

DAY 3

Jeremiah 31:35 _____

_____

Psalm 136:7-9 _____

_____

_____

John 1:1-5   Was Jesus just one of God's created beings? Explain.

_____

_____

_____

John 1:1-3   Did Jesus play a key role in creation?

_____

_____

_____

_____

Read Genesis 1:14-19 and study your memory verse.

Use this section to write down questions you may have from this week's passage:

_____

_____

_____

_____

Use this section to write down answers to your questions. Ask for help if needed.

_____

_____

_____

_____

Genesis 1:14-15 List all the things the lights are used for:

_____

_____

_____

_____

Name the great lights God created on day 4.

1. _____

2. _____

FUN FACT Did you know that everything God created was fully functional? For example, animals could have babies and trees could produce fruit right after God created them!

 Read Genesis 1:14-19 and study your memory verse.

DAY 5

Colossians 1:16   Explain: Why did God create all things?

_____

_____

God is eternal. This means that He has no beginning or end. Write out Psalm 90:2.

_____

_____

_____

God created seasons for us to enjoy.
Each season allows us to have new beginnings.

Read Genesis 8:22 and fill in the blanks.

While the earth remains, _____ and _____ ,

cold and heat, _____ and _____ , day and night,

shall not cease.

Read Genesis 1:14-19 and study your memory verse. Without looking, write down your memory verse.

DAY 6

_____

_____

_____

_____

Revelation 4:11 tells us, "Worthy are You, our LORD and our God, to receive glory and honor and power; for You created all things" (NASB). As you look at the specific details of the whale and falcon, think about how amazingly detailed the LORD was when He created everything. It should make us say, "Wow!"

BLUE WHALE
LARGEST ANIMAL ON EARTH

Their tongue weighs as much as an elephant!

80-100 feet long

Loudest animal on the planet

Lives to be about 80 years

average of 400,000 pounds

PEREGRINE FALCON
FASTEST ANIMAL IN THE WORLD

They can reach speeds of up to 200 miles per hour

14-19 inches long

Weight of about 2 pounds

Wingspan of 3 feet

Did you know? We know one day is a literal 24 hours. It is amazing how detailed God is with His creation! Think about how plants could survive for 24 hours without sunlight, but they could not live for millions of years without the sun. Plants need sunlight to survive. Plants were created on day 3 and the sun was created on day 4.

On the seventh day, "God rested from all his work" (Genesis 2:3). You've worked so hard this week—go and do the same!

DAY 7

ANSWER KEY

Here are some important answers to questions in the book. If an answer is not listed here, use your Bible to find the answer, or answer the question in your own words.

WEEK 4 ♦ DAY 3: *John 1:1–5* No. Jesus is eternal and is God. John 1:1 tells us that He has always been in existence. He is an equal person in the Trinity, which is what we call the three persons of God. The Father, Son, and Holy Spirit. *John 1:1–3* Yes, John 1:3 reminds us "all things were made through Him." ♦ **DAY 4:** *Genesis 1:14-15* seasons, days, years, and to bring light to the earth. *Great lights:* sun; *lights:* sun, moon ♦ **DAY 5:** *Colossians 1:16* for His glory.

WEEK 5

GENESIS 1:20-23

DAY 1

We don't know about you, but day 5 of creation is one of our favorites because we love ocean animals, marine life, and birds. Even to this day, some of our dreams include diving with sharks, swimming with dolphins, and watching sea turtle eggs hatch on the beach! These amazing creatures are all part of God's incredible design, causing different kinds of sea creatures and birds to fill the oceans and sky. Job reminds us, "But ask the . . . birds of the heavens, and they will tell you; or the bushes of the earth, and they will teach you; and the fish of the sea will declare to you. Who among all these does not know that the hand of the LORD has done this? In his hand is the life of every living thing" (Job 12:7-10).

In our study this week, you're going to read about God blessing these creatures and telling them to "be fruitful and multiply, and fill the waters in the seas, and let birds multiply on the earth" (Genesis 1:22). This means it was always God's plan for us to enjoy oceans and skies brimming with life! Isn't God so good?

| PRAY. | READ to understand, rather than race to the finish. | HIGHLIGHT who, what, and where. | CIRCLE key words and phrases you do not understand. | Add QUESTION MARKS next to anything confusing. | UNDERLINE important phrases and repetitive words. |

GENESIS 1:20-23

[20] And God said, "Let the waters swarm with swarms of living creatures, and let birds fly above the earth across the expanse of the heavens." [21] So God created the great sea creatures and every living creature that moves, with which the waters swarm, according to their kinds, and every winged bird according to its kind. And God saw that it was good. [22] And God blessed them, saying, "Be fruitful and multiply and fill the waters in the seas, and let birds multiply on the earth." [23] And there was evening and there was morning, the fifth day.

NOTES

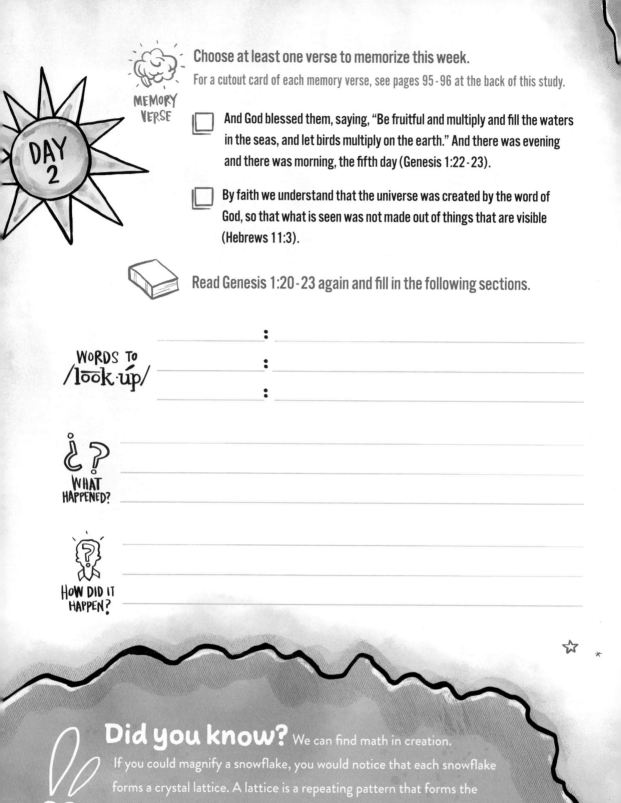

DAY 2

MEMORY VERSE

Choose at least one verse to memorize this week.

For a cutout card of each memory verse, see pages 95-96 at the back of this study.

☐ And God blessed them, saying, "Be fruitful and multiply and fill the waters in the seas, and let birds multiply on the earth." And there was evening and there was morning, the fifth day (Genesis 1:22-23).

☐ By faith we understand that the universe was created by the word of God, so that what is seen was not made out of things that are visible (Hebrews 11:3).

Read Genesis 1:20-23 again and fill in the following sections.

WORDS TO /lŏŏk·úp/

:_____

:_____

:_____

¿? WHAT HAPPENED?

_____

_____

_____

HOW DID IT HAPPEN?

_____

_____

☆ *

Did you know? We can find math in creation.

If you could magnify a snowflake, you would notice that each snowflake forms a crystal lattice. A lattice is a repeating pattern that forms the beautiful and unique shapes of each snowflake.

FUN FACT Think about how God has created something each day. It wasn't until day 5 that God created life. Life was created in a perfectly functioning and unique system.

Read Genesis 1:20-23 and study your memory verse.

Psalm 104:25 and Isaiah 27:1 are parallel passages to Genesis 1:20-23. Look up each passage and write it out.

DAY 3

Psalm 104:25 _____

_____

Isaiah 27:1 _____

_____

Explain or draw your greatest accomplishment.

DAY 4

Read Genesis 1:20-23 and study your memory verse.

Use this section to write down questions you may have from this week's passage:

_____

_____

_____

_____

Use this section to write down answers to your questions. Ask for help if needed.

_____

_____

_____

_____

The first time the word 🔑 **blessed** is used is in verse 22. Blessed means to give praise. God created life and the ability for life to multiply, and this deserved a blessing. God spoke directly to the creatures He created and blessed them. How neat! Describe a time when you were blessed or blessed someone else for something that you or they did.

Did you know?

The word for _birds_ mentioned in verse 22 means _flying things_ and would also include insects and flying reptiles.

_____

_____

_____

_____

_____

_____

Leviathan was one of the great sea creatures mentioned in verse 21. It is mentioned six times in the Bible and most of the passages talk about how God has complete control over this extinct creature of the sea. If you want to read more about the great Leviathan, read Job 41.

Read Genesis 1:20-23 and study your memory verse.

Read Job 41 then use this space to draw a Leviathan (use the ideas in Job, like a back made of rows of shields, flames from his mouth, smoke from his nostrils, not afraid of anything).

DAY 5

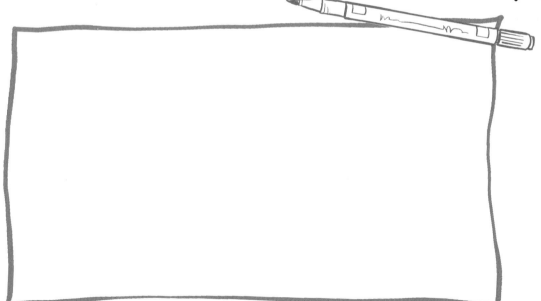

DAY 6

Read Genesis 1:20-23 and study your memory verse. Without looking, write down your memory verse.

_____

_____

_____

_____

_____

_____

Why is it important that God made plants and animals according to their own kind? Circle the answer.

A. The animals needed each other.

B. Adam and Eve wanted more than plants.

C. So they were kind to each other.

D. He was creating everything to reproduce and multiply.

We see the phrase "according to its kind" in verse 11. This is very important because it shows how God created a vast system of groups that have unique characteristics and reproduce within the boundaries of their kind. Animals can only breed with an animal in their "kind" group. Have you ever seen a zorse at the zoo? A zorse (male zebra and female horse) is possible because they are both from the same kind.

On the seventh day, "God rested from all his work" (Genesis 2:3). You've worked so hard this week—go and do the same!

DAY 7

ANSWER KEY

Here is an important answer to a question in the book. If an answer is not listed here, use your Bible to find the answer, or answer the question in your own words.

WEEK 5 DAY 6: *Multiple choice:* D

WEEK 6

DAY 1

We've reached a week that discusses the pinnacle of all creation. God not only created animals that walk the earth and all the creeping things, He created people in His image, which makes us more special than any other creature. Nothing else is said to be made in the image of God except mankind. God loves all His creation, but only humans had God breathe life into them. He made two genders, causing some to be born boys (male), and some to be born girls (female). The creation account details how God always intended for there to be just two genders. No matter what anyone might tell you, God's way is the best way. He wants girls to be girls, and boys to be boys. Both are created equal and special in their own unique way! God wants us to know our identity and the Bible teaches that we are unique among all living things because we are made in God's image.

As you consider God's perfect design in creation this week, remember this: God loves you so much and did not create you by accident. You were made on purpose and for a purpose! Psalm 18:30 reminds us, "God—his way is perfect; the word of the LORD proves true; he is a shield for all those who take refuge in him." God desires a relationship with those who are created in His image, and that relationship began when He made the first male and female.

NOTES

PRAY.

READ to understand, rather than race to the finish.

HIGHLIGHT who, what, and where.

CIRCLE key words and phrases you do not understand.

Add **QUESTION MARKS** next to anything confusing.

UNDERLINE important phrases and repetitive words.

GENESIS 1:24-31

24 And God said, "Let the earth bring forth living creatures according to their kinds—livestock and creeping things and beasts of the earth according to their kinds." And it was so. 25 And God made the beasts of the earth according to their kinds and the livestock according to their kinds, and everything that creeps on the ground according to its kind. And God saw that it was good. 26 Then God said, "Let us make man in our image, after our likeness. And let them have dominion over the fish of the sea and over the birds of the heavens and over the livestock and over all the earth and over every creeping thing that creeps on the earth."

27 So God created man in his own image, in the image of God he created him; male and female he created them. 28 And God blessed them. And God said to them, "Be fruitful and multiply and fill the earth and subdue it, and have dominion over the fish of the sea and over the birds of the heavens and over every living thing that moves on the earth." 29 And God said, "Behold, I have given you every plant yielding seed that is on the face of all the earth, and every tree with seed in its fruit. You shall have them for food. 30 And to every beast of the earth and to every bird of the heavens and to everything that creeps on the earth, everything that has the breath of life, I have given every green plant for food." And it was so. 31 And God saw everything that he had made, and behold, it was very good. And there was evening and there was morning, the sixth day.

MEMORY VERSE

Choose at least one verse to memorize this week.

For a cutout card of each memory verse, see pages 95 - 96 at the back of this study.

☐ Then God said, "Let us make man in our image, after our likeness. And let them have dominion over the fish…the birds…the livestock and over all the earth and over every creeping thing" (Genesis 1:26).

☐ So God created man in his own image, in the image of God he created him; male and female he created them (Genesis 1:27).

Read Genesis 1:24 - 31 again and fill in the following sections.

WORDS TO /lōōk·úp/

:

:

:

¿? WHAT HAPPENED?

HOW DID IT HAPPEN?

Did you know? Before the Fall, humans did not eat meat and animals did not hunt each other.

Read Genesis 1:24-31 and study your memory verse.

Psalm 8:6-8 and 1 Timothy 4:4 are parallel passages to Genesis 1:24-31.

Look up each passage and write it out.

DAY 3

Psalm 8:6-8 _____

_____

_____

1 Timothy 4:4 _____

_____

The word  **dominion** is a big way to say you have control over something. God did not give His authority over mankind's physical environment. He has total control over the planet, oceans, and atmosphere. There is only One who can make it rain, and that is our all-powerful God!

Genesis 1:26   What did God give man dominion over?

_____

_____

_____

DAY 4

Read Genesis 1:24-31 and study your memory verse.

Use this section to write down questions you may have from this week's passage:

Use this section to write down answers to your questions. Ask for help if needed.

Genesis 1:26 What is the importance of being created in God's image?

Read Ephesians 4:24. How is the likeness of God explained?

Read Genesis 1:24-31 and study your memory verse.

Read Genesis 1:27 and fill in the blanks.

So God created man in his own image, in the image of God he created him;

_____ and _____ he created them.

Genesis 1:27 explains how God created man and woman. This means that Eve was created on day 6 of creation, but we don't get to hear her remarkable story until Genesis 2.

DAY 5

Unscramble the words below and use them to fill in the blanks to answer the four things God told man and woman to do in Genesis 1:28.

eb   dna   lipymutl   illf   het   deusub   veah   mindinoo

1. _____ fruitful _____   _____ ☆

2. _____   _____ earth

3. _____ it

4. _____   _____ over the fish of the sea and
   over the birds of the heavens and over every living thing that moves on the earth

Genesis 1:29   What food did God give man to eat?

_____

_____

_____

_____

FUN FACT

Did you know dinosaurs were created on day 6 of creation?

DAY 6

Read Genesis 1:24-31 and study your memory verse.
Without looking, write down your memory verse.

_____

_____

_____

_____

_____

_____

What was created on each day?

Day 1: _____

Day 2: _____

Day 3: _____

Day 4: _____

Day 5: _____

Day 6: _____

Day 7: _____

Draw your favorite part of creation:

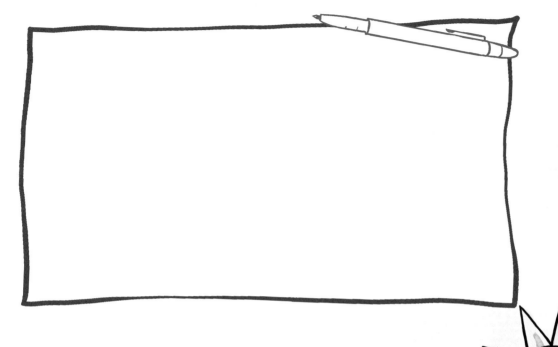

On the seventh day, "God rested from all his work" (Genesis 2:3). You've worked so hard this week—go and do the same!

ANSWER KEY

Here are some important answers to questions in the book. If an answer is not listed here, use your Bible to find the answer, or answer the question in your own words.

WEEK 6 DAY 3: *Genesis 1:26* (dominion) fish of the sea, birds of the heavens, livestock, all the earth, and every creeping thing ◊ *Genesis 1:26* (image) We were created to be a reflection of God, not like anything else created before. ◊ **DAY 5:** Unscramble: 1. Be, and, multiply; 2. Fill, the; 3. Subdue; 4. Have, dominion *Genesis 1:29* every plant and tree with seed in its fruit (we did not eat meat until the Fall) ◊ **DAY 6:** *Created each day;* Day 1: heavens, earth, light; Day 2: the expanse; Day 3: dry land and vegetation; Day 4: sun, moon, and stars; Day 5: sea creatures, flying creatures; Day 6: land animals, Adam, and Eve.

WEEK 7

GENESIS 2:1-3

DAY 1

This week we're going to learn why it's biblical to take a nap and get a good night's sleep! Okay, maybe not, but God provides an example of why rest is a good thing. On day 7 of creation, God doesn't rest because He was tired—He's way too powerful to ever get sleepy or weak. After creating all things, He rested to model for us that it was time to observe those things, enjoy those things, and take a break from work. God decided that out of the seven days of creation, He would work for six days, then dedicate one day as holy so that all of creation (especially humans) would worship Him! I don't know about you, but if there is a day that God has blessed, that is a day I want to enjoy!

PRAY.

READ to understand, rather than race to the finish.

HIGHLIGHT who, what, and where.

CIRCLE key words and phrases you do not understand.

Add QUESTION MARKS next to anything confusing.

UNDERLINE important phrases and repetitive words.

GENESIS 2:1-3

[1] Thus the heavens and the earth were finished, and all the host of them. [2] And on the seventh day God finished his work that he had done, and he rested on the seventh day from all his work that he had done. [3] So God blessed the seventh day and made it holy, because on it God rested from all his work that he had done in creation.

NOTES

DAY 2

Choose at least one verse to memorize this week.

For a cutout card of each memory verse, see pages 95-96 at the back of this study.

☐ So God blessed the seventh day and made it holy, because on it God rested from all his work that he had done in creation (Genesis 2:3).

☐ Remember the Sabbath day, to keep it holy. Six days you shall labor, and do all your work, but the seventh day is a Sabbath to the LORD your God. On it you shall not do any work (Exodus 20:8-10).

Read Genesis 2:1-3 again and fill in the following sections.

WORDS TO /lŏŏk·úp/

: _____

: _____

: _____

¿? WHAT HAPPENED?

_____

_____

_____

HOW DID IT HAPPEN?

_____

_____

_____

Did you know? God created the universe, including 200 sextillion stars in six actual days. Now that is some serious speed and power—and a lot of zeroes!

200,000,000,000,000,000,000,000

Read Genesis 2:1-3 and study your memory verse.

Exodus 20:11 and Mark 2:27-28 are parallel passages to Genesis 2:1-3.
Look up each passage and write it out.

Exodus 20:11 _____

_____

_____

Mark 2:27-28 _____

_____

_____

Read Genesis 2:3 and fill in the blanks.

So God _____ the seventh day and made it _____ ,

because on it God _____ from all his work that he had done in

_____ .

Colossians 1:16, Revelation 4:11   Why were all things created?

_____

_____

_____

1 Corinthians 10:31   How are we to do everything?

_____

_____

_____

Read Genesis 2:1 - 3 and study your memory verse.

Use this section to write down questions you may have from this week's passage:

_____

_____

_____

_____

Use this section to write down answers to your questions. Ask for help if needed.

_____

_____

_____

_____

Genesis 2:3   **Explain why God blessed the seventh day and made it holy.**

_____

_____

_____

_____

The earth is about 6,000–10,000 years old.

Read Genesis 2:1-3 and study your memory verse.

Genesis 1:31   **Were Adam and Eve good when God created them?**

_____

_____

"All the host of them" refers to the sun, moon, stars—all created on days 5 and 6. (Genesis 2:1).

How long did it take for God to create everything? (See Genesis 2:1-2.) Circle the answer.

A. Eternity

B. 144 hours

C. 6 days

D. B. and C.

Through creation we see that God is **sovereign.** Sovereignty means God is Lord (God rules) over all creation. Take great comfort knowing the Lord is in control of all things! Colossians 1:16-17 tells us, "For by him all things were created, in heaven and on earth, visible and invisible, whether thrones or dominions or rulers or authorities—all things were created through him and for him. And he is before all things, and in him all things hold together."

Complete the crossword puzzle below.

ACROSS

4. Adam and Eve were not to eat from the tree of _____

5. The first man created by God

7. The first book of the Bible

9. The day when God created light

DOWN

1. Adam and Eve lived in the garden of _____

2. The act of God bringing the universe into existence

3. What God created on the second day

6. The seventh day was a day of _____

8. The woman created from Adam's rib

9. God created these on the fifth day

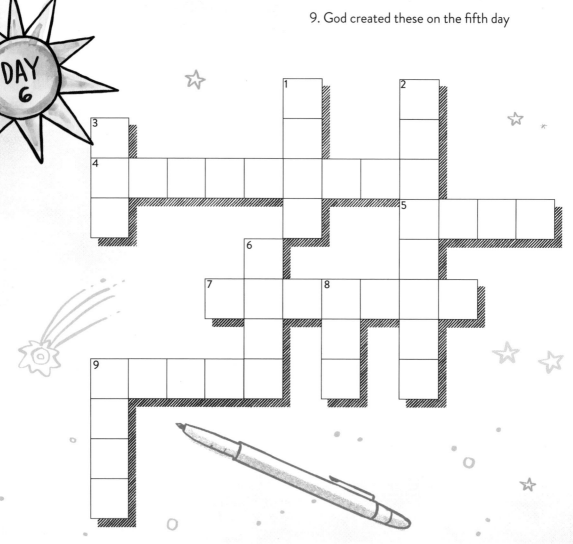

Read Genesis 2:1-3 and study your memory verse.
Without looking, write down your memory verse.

_____

_____

_____

About how old is the earth? Circle the answer.

A. 1–2 million years old

B. 4–10 billion years old

C. 6,000–10,000 years old

D. 120,000–150,000

DAY 7

On the seventh day, "God rested from all his work" (Genesis 2:3).
You've worked so hard this week—go and do the same!

ANSWER KEY

Here are some important answers to questions in the book. If an answer is not listed here, use your Bible to find the answer, or answer the question in your own words.

WEEK 7 DAY 3: Colossians 1:16; Revelation 4:11 for God and His glory ◇ **DAY 4:** Genesis 2:3 God chose to rest from His work on the seventh day, and so He created an example for us to follow for all other weeks. ◇ **DAY 5:** Genesis 1:31 Yes. When God created Adam and Eve they did not yet have their eyes opened to evil and had never sinned. _Multiple choice:_ D 1 Corinthians 1:16-17 All for the glory of God! ◇ **DAY 6:** _Crossword: Across_ 4. knowledge; 5. Adam; 7. Genesis; 9. first. _Down_ 1. Eden; 2. creation; 3. sky; 6. rest; 8. Eve; 9. fish. _Multiple choice:_ C

WEEK 8

GENESIS 2:4-25

Do you have any pets? If so, how did you come up with their name? If you don't have a pet, think about what kind of pet you would want and what you would name it! That's exactly what Adam had to do when God gave him a special job to name all the animals in creation!

After Adam named the animals, God decided Adam needed a helper and a partner for life. God created Eve from Adam's rib and thus created one of the most important relationships we can ever have in life. This week we will learn how God brought Adam and Eve together for the first marriage ever! God cares so much about marriage—it is a reflection of His love for us. He also made marriage so important, that a male and a female who get married are called to stay together as one team, just as Mark 10:9 states, "what therefore God has joined together, let not man separate."

PRAY.

READ to understand, rather than race to the finish.

HIGHLIGHT who, what, and where.

CIRCLE key words and phrases you do not understand.

Add QUESTION MARKS next to anything confusing.

UNDERLINE important phrases and repetitive words.

4 These are the generations of the heavens and the earth when they were created, in the day that the Lord God made the earth and the heavens. 5 When no bush of the field was yet in the land and no small plant of the field had yet sprung up—for the Lord God had not caused it to rain on the land, and there was no man to work the ground, 6 and a mist was going up from the land and was watering the whole face of the ground—7 then the Lord God formed the man of dust from the ground and breathed into his nostrils the breath of life, and the man became a living creature. 8 And the Lord God planted a garden in Eden, in the east, and there he put the man whom he had formed. 9 And out of the ground the Lord God made to spring up every tree that is pleasant to the sight and good for food. The tree of life was in the midst of the garden, and the tree of the knowledge of good and evil. 10 A river flowed out of Eden to water the garden, and there it divided and became four rivers… 15 The Lord God took the man and put him in the garden of Eden to work it and keep it. 16 And the Lord God commanded the man, saying, "You may surely eat of every tree of the garden, 17 but of the tree of the knowledge of good and evil you shall not eat, for in the day that you eat of it you shall surely die." 18 Then the Lord God said, "It is not good that the man should be alone; I will make him a helper fit for him." 19 Now out of the ground the Lord God had formed every beast of the field and every bird of the heavens and brought them to the man to see what he would call them. And whatever the man called every living creature, that was its name. 20 The man gave names to all livestock and to the birds of the heavens and to every beast of the field. But for Adam there was not found a helper fit for him. 21 So the Lord God caused a deep sleep to fall upon the man, and while he slept took one of his ribs and closed up its place with flesh. 22 And the rib that the Lord God had taken from the man he made into a woman and brought her to the man. 23 Then the man said, "This at last is bone of my bones and flesh of my flesh; she shall be called Woman, because she was taken out of Man." 24 Therefore a man shall leave his father and his mother and hold fast to his wife, and they shall become one flesh. 25 And the man and his wife were both naked and were not ashamed.

MEMORY VERSE

Choose at least one verse to memorize this week.

For a cutout card of each memory verse, see pages 95-96 at the back of this study.

☐ The LORD God formed the man of dust from the ground and breathed into his nostrils the breath of life, and the man became a living creature (Genesis 2:7).

☐ This at last is bone of my bones and flesh of my flesh; she shall be called Woman, because she was taken out of Man (Genesis 2:23).

Read Genesis 2:4-25 again and fill in the following sections.

WORDS TO /lŏŏk·úp/

_____ : _____
_____ : _____
_____ : _____

**¿?
WHAT HAPPENED?**

_____
_____
_____

HOW DID IT HAPPEN?

_____
_____
_____

Did you know? The Bible tells us that death and suffering come because of the Fall. Before the Fall there was no death or disease. The world was in perfect harmony. Death came because of the original sin of Adam and Eve. Imagine how wonderful the Garden of Eden must have been before the Fall!

Read Genesis 2:4-25 and study your memory verse.

1 Timothy 2:13, Romans 6:23, and Psalm 139:14 are parallel passages to Genesis 2:4-25. Look up each passage and write it out.

DAY 3

1 Timothy 2:13 _____

_____

Romans 6:23 _____

_____

Psalm 139:14 _____

_____

Draw a picture of Eden.

Genesis 2:6 How was the land being watered?

_____

_____

Read Genesis 2:4-25 and study your memory verse.

Use this section to write down questions you may have from this week's passage:

_____

_____

_____

_____

Use this section to write down answers to your questions. Ask for help if needed.

_____

_____

_____

_____

Genesis 2:7   How did God create man?

_____

_____

_____

_____

Psalm 121:7 (NASB)   When God created man, He not only gave him a body but also a soul. What will God do to our soul?

_____

_____

Read Genesis 2:4-25 and study your memory verse.

DAY 5

Genesis 2:15   Why did God put man in the Garden of Eden?

_____

_____

_____

Genesis 2:16-17   What command did God give man in verses 16 and 17?

_____

_____

_____

Genesis 2:18   What did God say before He created the animals?

_____

_____

_____

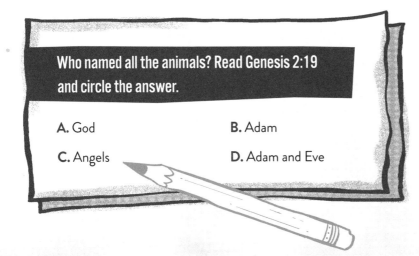

Who named all the animals? Read Genesis 2:19 and circle the answer.

A. God   **B.** Adam

C. Angels   **D.** Adam and Eve

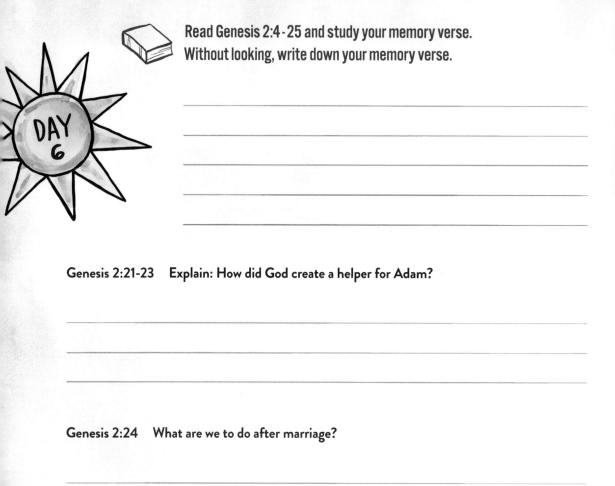

Read Genesis 2:4-25 and study your memory verse.
Without looking, write down your memory verse.

DAY 6

_____

_____

_____

_____

_____

Genesis 2:21-23   Explain: How did God create a helper for Adam?

_____

_____

_____

Genesis 2:24   What are we to do after marriage?

_____

_____

_____

Genesis 2:25   Adam and Eve were both naked and not ashamed.
Why were they unashamed and innocent?

_____

_____

On the seventh day, "God rested from all his work" (Genesis 2:3). You've worked so hard this week—go and do the same!

DAY 7

ANSWER KEY

Here are some important answers to questions in the book. If an answer is not listed here, use your Bible to find the answer, or answer the question in your own words.

WEEK 8 **DAY 3:** *Genesis 2:6* from a mist ◊ **DAY 4:** *Genesis 2:7* God created man from the dust of the ground. He breathed life into his nostrils. *Psalm 121:7* He will keep (protect) your soul. ◊ **DAY 5:** *Genesis 2:15* to work it and keep it *Genesis 2:18* "It is not good that the man should be alone." *Multiple Choice:* B ◊ **DAY 6:** *Genesis 2:24* leave our father and mother and become one flesh with our spouse *Genesis 2:25* They did not have any knowledge of evil. Before the Fall, nakedness would not bring shame. It was innocent.

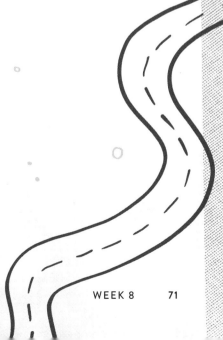

WEEK 9

GENESIS 3:1-13

DAY 1

Have you ever made something only to see it ruined by someone else?
Imagine building a Lego plane, doing a puzzle, or even making a fort, but after all your hard work, someone comes in and takes it apart. This would likely be frustrating for you. It happens to everyone at some point in their life. Well, in the Garden of Eden, after God said that everything was good, someone came and ruined the perfection of creation by tempting Adam and Eve to sin and disobey God. **Sin** means to miss the mark or target. When we say, do, or think something that is our way and not God's way, it is considered sin. The one who tempted Adam and Eve is named Satan. He's also known as the devil, Lucifer (Isaiah 14:12 KJV), tempter, the evil one, and a roaring lion (1 Peter 5:8).

The Bible teaches that Satan is a fallen angel, who once was highly regarded in heaven, only to be cast down from heaven by God because he was jealous and wanted to be more powerful than God. In anger and rebellion, he wanted to destroy what God so beautifully made and destroy mankind in the process. As the father of lies, he was able to deceive Eve by causing her to doubt God's instructions in the garden. In a moment of weakness, Adam and Eve sinned against God, and just like many of us, they wanted to hide after they had done something wrong. The result was disastrous, they became very ashamed, and their relationship with God was forever broken by sin.

PRAY.

READ to understand.

HIGHLIGHT who, what, and where.

CIRCLE key words and phrases.

Add QUESTION MARKS.

UNDERLINE important and repetitive words.

[1] Now the serpent was more crafty than any other beast of the field that the Lord God had made. He said to the woman, "Did God actually say, 'You shall not eat of any tree in the garden'?" [2] And the woman said to the serpent, "We may eat of the fruit of the trees in the garden, [3] but God said, 'You shall not eat of the fruit of the tree that is in the midst of the garden, neither shall you touch it, lest you die.'" [4] But the serpent said to the woman, "You will not surely die. [5] For God knows that when you eat of it your eyes will be opened, and you will be like God, knowing good and evil." [6] So when the woman saw that the tree was good for food, and that it was a delight to the eyes, and that the tree was to be desired to make one wise, she took of its fruit and ate, and she also gave some to her husband who was with her, and he ate. [7] Then the eyes of both were opened, and they knew that they were naked. And they sewed fig leaves together and made themselves loincloths. [8] And they heard the sound of the Lord God walking in the garden in the cool of the day, and the man and his wife hid themselves from the presence of the Lord God among the trees of the garden. [9] But the Lord God called to the man and said to him, "Where are you?" [10] And he said, "I heard the sound of you in the garden, and I was afraid, because I was naked, and I hid myself." [11] He said, "Who told you that you were naked? Have you eaten of the tree of which I commanded you not to eat?" [12] The man said, "The woman whom you gave to be with me, she gave me fruit of the tree, and I ate." [13] Then the Lord God said to the woman, "What is this that you have done?" The woman said, "The serpent deceived me, and I ate."

NOTES

_____

_____

_____

_____

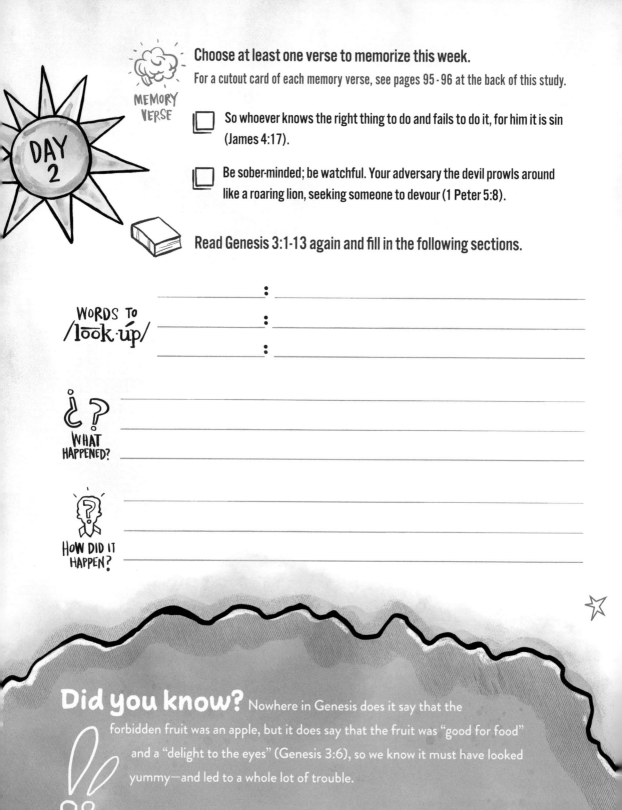

DAY 2

Choose at least one verse to memorize this week.
For a cutout card of each memory verse, see pages 95 - 96 at the back of this study.

MEMORY VERSE

☐ So whoever knows the right thing to do and fails to do it, for him it is sin (James 4:17).

☐ Be sober-minded; be watchful. Your adversary the devil prowls around like a roaring lion, seeking someone to devour (1 Peter 5:8).

Read Genesis 3:1-13 again and fill in the following sections.

WORDS TO /lŏŏk-úp/

: _____
: _____
: _____

¿?
WHAT HAPPENED?

_____
_____
_____
_____

HOW DID IT HAPPEN?

_____
_____
_____

Did you know? Nowhere in Genesis does it say that the forbidden fruit was an apple, but it does say that the fruit was "good for food" and a "delight to the eyes" (Genesis 3:6), so we know it must have looked yummy—and led to a whole lot of trouble.

Read Genesis 3:1-13 and study your memory verse.

John 8:44, Romans 5:12, and Isaiah 53:6 are parallel passages to Genesis 3:1-13.

Look up each passage and write it out.

DAY 3

John 8:44 _____

_____

_____

Romans 5:12 _____

_____

_____

Isaiah 53:6 _____

_____

_____

James 4:17   **Based on this verse, explain what sin is.**

_____

_____

_____

Read Genesis 3:1-13 and study your memory verse.

Use this section to write down questions you may have from this week's passage:

_____

_____

_____

_____

Use this section to write down answers to your questions. Ask for help if needed.

_____

_____

_____

_____

Q+A

Did Adam and Eve go to heaven? **Heaven** is the future home of believers. There will be no death or pain. Read Genesis 4:25-26 before you read the answer below.

Answer: Though the Bible doesn't specifically say, there are some clues that help us answer this question. Genesis 4:3-5 does tell us that the sons of Adam and Eve brought offerings to the Lord. "Cain brought an offering to the LORD from the fruit of the ground. Abel, on his part also brought an offering, from the firstborn of his flock and from their fat portions. And the LORD had regard for Abel and his offering; but for Cain and his offering He had no regard" (NASB). This doesn't guarantee anything for Adam and Eve, but it does show that they taught their children the ways of the Lord.

Genesis 3:1-4 Satan knew he could not kill man but what could he do to hurt him?

_____

_____

_____

_____

Read Genesis 3:1-13 and study your memory verse.

DAY 5

Genesis 3:7   What happened when Adam and Eve sinned?

_____

_____

_____

Genesis 3:12   What did Adam say to God in this passage?

_____

_____

_____

Genesis 3:13   What did Eve say to God in this passage?

_____

_____

_____

Read Genesis 3:1-13 and study your memory verse. Without looking, write down your memory verse.

_____

_____

Read James 1:13-15: [13] Let no one say when he is tempted, "I am being tempted by God," for God cannot be tempted with evil, and he himself tempts no one. [14] But each person is tempted when he is lured and enticed by his own desire. [15] Then desire when it has conceived gives birth to sin, and sin when it is fully grown brings forth death.

Notice how this pattern works:
Step 1: Temptation → Step 2: Sin → Step 3: Death

Now, draw a line to connect the items on the left with the matching definitions on the right.

Satan   knowing the right thing to do but not doing it

sin   the father of lies who comes to steal, kill, and destroy

temptation   a desire to do something wrong

Ephesians 2:3   Explain: When did we become sinful?

_____

Read Jeremiah 17:9 and fill in the blanks.

The _____ is _____ above all

things, and _____ sick; who can understand it?

On the seventh day, "God rested from all his work" (Genesis 2:3).
You've worked so hard this week—go and do the same!

DAY 7

ANSWER KEY

Here are some important answers to questions in the book. If an answer is not listed here, use
your Bible to find the answer, or answer the question in your own words.

WEEK 9 DAY 4: *Genesis 3:1-4* Satan lied and made Eve doubt God. ◇ **DAY 5:** *Genesis 3:7* They were no longer
unashamed and now knew evil. *Genesis 3:13* Eve blamed the serpent. ◇ **DAY 6:** Draw a line: Satan > father of lies; sin > knowing/not doing; temptation > desire *Ephesians 2:3* He blamed God for giving him Eve. *Genesis 3:12*
We are born sinful, "by nature children of wrath."

WEEK 10

GENESIS 3:14-24

DAY 1

This is one of the most important chapters for us to understand even though it may contain one of the most uncomfortable truths. If you stick with it, we promise there is hope just ahead!

After Adam and Eve sinned, there were consequences. Just like there will be consequences if someone cheats on a test, lies, or hurts someone else. **Consequences** are results of our actions. God chose that there would be consequences for sin since sin separates us from Him and hurts other people. Numbers 32:23 says our sin will find us out. For Adam, there were certain consequences. For Eve, there would be other consequences. These are not only meant to be a punishment for sin, but they are also meant to point us to the solution found in the Good News about Jesus Christ. Here is a big HINT: There is a way to be free from the punishment of sin and totally forgiven! But first, let's understand how serious sin is and why it harms our relationship with God.

PRAY.

READ to understand, rather than race to the finish.

HIGHLIGHT who, what, and where.

CIRCLE key words and phrases you do not understand.

Add **QUESTION MARKS** next to anything confusing.

UNDERLINE important phrases and repetitive words.

¹⁴ The Lord God said to the serpent, "Because you have done this, cursed are you above all livestock and above all beasts of the field; on your belly you shall go, and dust you shall eat all the days of your life. ¹⁵ I will put enmity between you and the woman, and between your offspring and her offspring; he shall bruise your head, and you shall bruise his heel." ¹⁶ To the woman he said, "I will surely multiply your pain in childbearing; in pain you shall bring forth children. Your desire shall be contrary to your husband, but he shall rule over you." ¹⁷ And to Adam he said, "Because you have listened to the voice of your wife and have eaten of the tree of which I commanded you, 'You shall not eat of it,' cursed is the ground because of you; in pain you shall eat of it all the days of your life; ¹⁸ thorns and thistles it shall bring forth for you; and you shall eat the plants of the field. ¹⁹ By the sweat of your face you shall eat bread, till you return to the ground, for out of it you were taken; for you are dust, and to dust you shall return." ²⁰ The man called his wife's name Eve, because she was the mother of all living. ²¹ And the Lord God made for Adam and for his wife garments of skins and clothed them. ²² Then the Lord God said, "Behold, the man has become like one of us in knowing good and evil. Now, lest he reach out his hand and take also of the tree of life and eat, and live forever—" ²³ therefore the Lord God sent him out from the garden of Eden to work the ground from which he was taken. ²⁴ He drove out the man, and at the east of the garden of Eden he placed the cherubim and a flaming sword that turned every way to guard the way to the tree of life.

NOTES

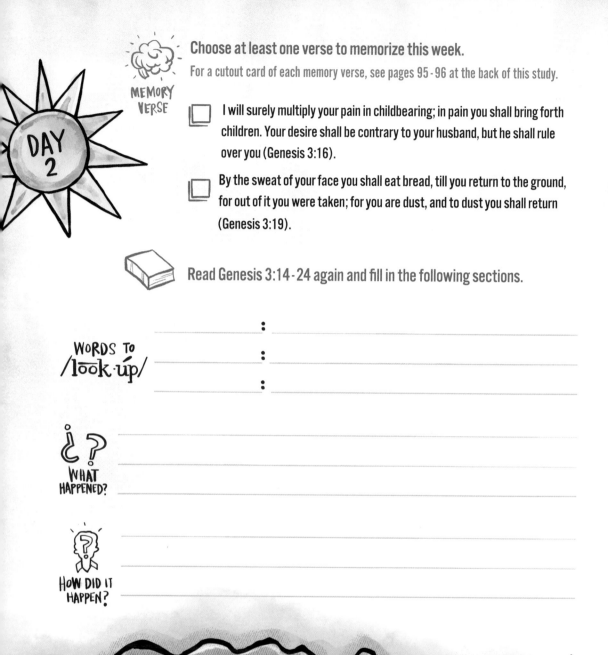

DAY 2

Choose at least one verse to memorize this week.

For a cutout card of each memory verse, see pages 95-96 at the back of this study.

MEMORY VERSE

☐ I will surely multiply your pain in childbearing; in pain you shall bring forth children. Your desire shall be contrary to your husband, but he shall rule over you (Genesis 3:16).

☐ By the sweat of your face you shall eat bread, till you return to the ground, for out of it you were taken; for you are dust, and to dust you shall return (Genesis 3:19).

Read Genesis 3:14-24 again and fill in the following sections.

WORDS TO /lo͞ok·úp/

_____ : _____

_____ : _____

_____ : _____

¿? WHAT HAPPENED?

_____

_____

_____

HOW DID IT HAPPEN?

_____

_____

_____

Did you know? Satan is not a serpent, even though he spoke through one when he tempted Eve. He is actually a fallen angel (Ezekiel 28:12-17).

Read Genesis 3:14-24 and study your memory verse.

1 Corinthians 11:3, Proverbs 1:7-10, and Ecclesiastes 7:20 are parallel passages to Genesis 3:14-24. Look up each passage and write it out.

DAY 3

1 Corinthians 11:3

Proverbs 1:7-10

Ecclesiastes 7:20

Explain: Who sins?

DAY 4

Read Genesis 3:14-24 and study your memory verse.

Use this section to write down questions you may have from this week's passage:

_____

_____

_____

_____

Use this section to write down answers to your questions.
Ask for help if needed.

_____

_____

_____

_____

1 John 1:8-10   How should we respond when we sin?

_____

_____

_____

Psalm 119:11   Explain: What will help with avoiding sin?

_____

_____

_____

Read Genesis 3:14-24 and study your memory verse.

When we choose to go our way instead of God's way it is called **sin**. There are always consequences when we sin.

Ezra 9:6   What are the two consequences of our sin?

1. _____

2. _____

Isaiah 59:2   Explain: What separates man from God?

_____

_____

_____

Romans 5:12-14   Explain: How did death enter the world?

_____

_____

Read 1 Corinthians 15:22 and fill in the blanks.

For as in Adam all _____ , so also in Christ shall all be made _____ .

1 Corinthians 10:13   Is there a temptation that is too hard for us to handle?

_____

_____

_____

DAY 6

Read Genesis 3:14-24 and study your memory verse.
Without looking, write down your memory verse.

_____

_____

_____

James 4:1-2 (NASB)   What is the cause of our fighting and evil desires?

_____

Just as eating the fruit in the garden seemed like a good idea in the beginning, often sin can be the same way. Think of a time when you were tempted and sinned. What consequences followed?

_____

_____

Proverbs 16:18 says, " _____ goes before destruction, and a

_____ _____ before a fall."

What sin are you struggling with that you would like to be free from?

_____

_____

While it is true that sin can bring much pain and destruction, God does not send all sinners to hell. Hope is found in John 3:16. "For God so loved the world, that he gave his only Son, that whoever believes in him should not perish but have eternal life." Only a holy God can provide eternal life. **Holy** means set apart, exalted above all. God is perfect and without sin.

On the seventh day, "God rested from all his work" (Genesis 2:3). You've worked so hard this week—go and do the same!

DAY 7

ANSWER KEY

Here are some important answers to questions in the book. If an answer is not listed here, use your Bible to find the answer, or answer the question in your own words.

WEEK 10 DAY 4: 1 John 1:8-10   We should confess our sin (repent).   Psalm 119:11   Knowing God's Word will help us to resist sin. ◇ **DAY 5:** Ezra 9:6   1. Shame; 2. Guilt.   Isaiah 59:2   Sin   Romans 5:12   through Adam's sin   1 Corinthians 10:13 No! ◇ **DAY 6:** James 4:1-2   lust and envy

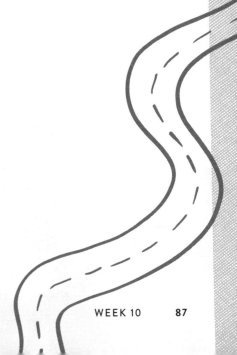

EPIC-logue

Can you remember a time when it rained so much that it made the next sunny day even more special? It is the rainy days that help us appreciate the sunny days. The same thing can be said regarding sin's bad news (rainy day!) helping us appreciate the good news about forgiveness and salvation (sunny day!). **Salvation** is deliverance from sin and its consequences. We receive salvation from God when we place our faith in Jesus Christ because of His **sacrifice** for our sin. A sacrifice is when something is given up for the benefit of another.

We know sin is bad news. Sin is serious and causes destruction! But once we understand how bad sin is, it causes us to appreciate how amazing forgiveness is! Even though mankind sinned and there had to be consequences, God sent His own Son, Jesus, to die as a sacrifice for sin. Jesus made **atonement** for our sin—this means He shed His blood to pay for our sins and took the full punishment of God's wrath in our place. When we **repent**—which means to change our mind and turn away from sin—we are agreeing with God that sin is serious. Beyond repentance (which is good), when we place our faith in Jesus Christ and trust in Him to be the One who washed away our sin, we are forgiven and we experience salvation! Romans 8:1 says, "Therefore, there is now no condemnation for those who are in Christ" (NIV). This passage means that even though there are consequences for sin, the punishment for sin is no longer something you will suffer forever. This is the grace of God to us! **Grace** means "unmerited favor," which means that we don't do anything to earn salvation, we simply have faith in Jesus and God does the rest!

Read the following passage together and discuss how sinners receive grace and **mercy** through Jesus Christ's sacrifice.

Mercy is love or compassion that is shown even though we are undeserving.

[1] And you were dead in the trespasses and sins [2] in which you once walked, following the course of this world, following the prince of the power of the air, the spirit that is now at work in the sons of disobedience— [3] among whom we all once lived in the passions of our flesh, carrying out the desires of the body and the mind, and were by nature children of wrath, like the rest of mankind. [4] But God, being rich in mercy, because of the great love with which he loved us, [5] even when we were dead in our trespasses, made us alive together with Christ—by grace you have been saved— [6] and raised us up with him and seated us with him in the heavenly places in Christ Jesus, [7] so that in the coming ages he might show the immeasurable riches of his grace in kindness toward us in Christ Jesus. [8] For by grace you have been saved through faith. And this is not your own doing; it is the gift of God, [9] not a result of works, so that no one may boast. [10] For we are his workmanship, created in Christ Jesus for good works, which God prepared beforehand, that we should walk in them.

Discuss and answer the following questions together.

Ephesians 6:10-18   What are some things we can do to avoid sin? We will never be sinless, but we must try our best to avoid sin.

Bonus! Here are two more memory verse options for you.

MEMORY VERSE

☐ For by grace you have been saved through faith. And this is not your own doing; it is the gift of God (Ephesians 2:8).

☐ For we are his workmanship, created in Christ Jesus for good works, which God prepared beforehand, that we should walk in them (Ephesians 2:10).

Read John 3:16, Romans 5:8, Romans 6:23, Romans 8:1, Romans 10:9, 2 Corinthians 5:21, and Ephesians 2:8. Based on those verses but in your own words, how would you explain the gospel?

_____

_____

_____

_____

How are we to live once we follow Christ?

Colossians 3:2

Set your minds on things that are _____ not on things that are

on _____ .

Galatians 5:22-23

But the fruit of the Spirit is _____ , joy, peace, _____ ,

kindness, goodness, _____ , gentleness, self-control.

Ephesians 4:29

Let no _____ talk come out of your mouths, but only such as is good

for _____ , as fits the occasion, that it may give _____ to those

who hear.

Ephesians 4:32

Be _____ to one another, tenderhearted, _____ one another,

as God in _____ forgave you.

Colossians 1:10

So as to walk in a manner _____ of the Lord, fully pleasing to him:

_____ in every good work and increasing in the _____ of God.

One last thing, remember that God made the world perfect!

Sin ruined that perfection and separated us from God,

but salvation came through Jesus Christ and we can be

made right with God again! Live with that hope in mind!

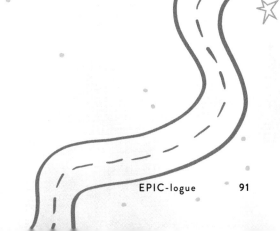

Key Words 🗝

Atonement: Jesus atoned for sin when He shed His blood to pay for our sins, taking the full punishment of God's wrath in our place (Romans 5:6-8).

Blessed: This means "to give praise" (Genesis 1:22).

Consequence: We reap what we sow, and a consequence is a result of our actions (Galatians 6:7).

Created: This means "to make something new" (Genesis 1:1).

Dominion: This word means "to have control over something" (Genesis 1:26).

Elohim: This is the Hebrew word for God, which means "mighty and powerful one" (Genesis 1:1).

Eternal: This word means there is no beginning, end, or advancement of time (Psalm 90:2).

Gospel: The Good News explains Jesus's sinless life, sacrificial death, and divine resurrection—all of which allows for our sins to be forgiven and eternal life to be our future (John 3:16-17).

Grace: This means "unmerited favor or kindness." We don't do anything to earn grace, it is a gift from God to those of us who are undeserving. Grace frees us from burdens and gives eternal life (Ephesians 2:8-9).

Heaven: This is the future home of believers. There will be no death or pain (Revelation 21:1-4).

Holy: God is set apart, exalted above all. God is perfect and without sin (1 Samuel 2:2).

Hovered: This means "a gentle flutter" (Genesis 1:2).

Mercy: This means to love or show compassion. God gives us mercy even though we are undeserving of it (Ephesians 2:4-5).

Repent: We turn the other way. We change our mind. When we truly repent, there will also be a change of actions (2 Chronicles 7:14).

Sacrifice: This means something is given up for the benefit of another. Jesus gave His life so that we would be given mercy and forgiveness from our sins (John 3:16).

Salvation: Jesus made a way for salvation—deliverance from sin and its consequences. We receive salvation from God when we place our faith in Jesus Christ because of His sacrifice for our sin (Romans 3:25-28).

Sin: To sin is to miss the mark or target. When we say, do, or think something that is our way and not God's way, it is considered sin (James 4:17).

Sovereign: This refers to God ruling over all creation (Colossians 1:16-17).

ABOUT THE AUTHORS

Costi and Christyne Hinn are the authors of the children's books *In Jesus' Name I Pray* and the Fruit-of-the-Spirit Tale series, including *The King Who Found His Self-Control* and *The Farmer Who Chose to Plant Kindness*. Costi is the teaching pastor at Shepherd's House Bible Church in Chandler, Arizona, and president of For the Gospel, an online resource ministry that provides sound doctrine for everyday people. Christyne pours her time into her family, her church, and writing. They are the joyful parents of six children.

Memory Verse Cutouts

*Here are your memory verse cutout cards.
Each week has two options: one on the front
of the card and the other on the back.*

week 1

In the beginning, God created
the heavens and the earth.

GENESIS 1:1

week 2

In the beginning was the Word, and the Word
was with God, and the Word was God.
He was in the beginning with God.

JOHN 1:1-2

week 3

The earth is the LORD's and the fullness thereof,
the world and those who dwell therein.

PSALM 24:1

week 4

Let there be lights in the expanse of the heavens to
separate the day from the night. And let them be
for signs and for seasons, and for days and years.

GENESIS 1:14

week 5

And God blessed them, saying, "Be fruitful
and multiply and fill the waters in the seas, and
let birds multiply on the earth." And there was
evening and there was morning, the fifth day.

GENESIS 1:22-23

week 6

Then God said, "Let us make man in our image,
after our likeness. And let them have dominion
over the fish...the birds...the livestock and over all
the earth and over every creeping thing."

GENESIS 1:26

week 7

So God blessed the seventh day and made it
holy, because on it God rested from all his
work that he had done in creation.

GENESIS 2:3

week 8

The LORD God formed the man of dust from the
ground and breathed into his nostrils the breath
of life, and the man became a living creature.

GENESIS 2:7

week 9

So whoever knows the right thing to do
and fails to do it, for him it is sin.

JAMES 4:17

week 10

I will surely multiply your pain in childbearing; in pain
you shall bring forth children. Your desire shall be
contrary to your husband, but he shall rule over you.

GENESIS 3:16

BONUS

For by grace you have been saved
through faith. And this is not your
own doing; it is the gift of God.

EPHESIANS 2:8

week 1

And God saw everything that he had made, and behold, it was very good.

GENESIS 1:31

Memory Verse Cutouts

These are the second memory verse options for each week. Choose one to memorize, or you can memorize both!

week 3

The sea is His, for it was He who made it, And His hands formed the dry land.

PSALM 95:5 NASB

week 2

Let them praise the name of the LORD! For he commanded and they were created.

PSALM 148:5

week 5

By faith we understand that the universe was created by the word of God, so that what is seen was not made out of things that are visible.

HEBREWS 11:3

week 4

To him who made the great lights, for his steadfast love endures forever.

PSALM 136:7

week 7

Remember the Sabbath day, to keep it holy. Six days you shall labor, and do all your work, but the seventh day is a Sabbath to the LORD your God. On it you shall not do any work.

EXODUS 20:8-10

week 6

So God created man in his own image, in the image of God he created him; male and female he created them.

GENESIS 1:27

week 9

Be sober-minded; be watchful. Your adversary the devil prowls around like a roaring lion, seeking someone to devour.

1 PETER 5:8

week 8

This at last is bone of my bones and flesh of my flesh; she shall be called Woman, because she was taken out of Man.

GENESIS 2:23

BONUS

For we are his workmanship, created in Christ Jesus for good works, which God prepared beforehand, that we should walk in them.

EPHESIANS 2:10

week 10

By the sweat of your face you shall eat bread, till you return to the ground, for out of it you were taken; for you are dust, and to dust you shall return.

GENESIS 3:19